Three Bakers
& a Loon

Written by: Allison Boris & Karen Jacobs
Illustrated by: Allison Boris

ISBN: 978-0-9850440-2-2

First edition 2013

Printed in the United States of America

Dedication

Dedicated to exceptional children everywhere.

Ding Dong!

Who is at the door?

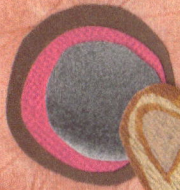

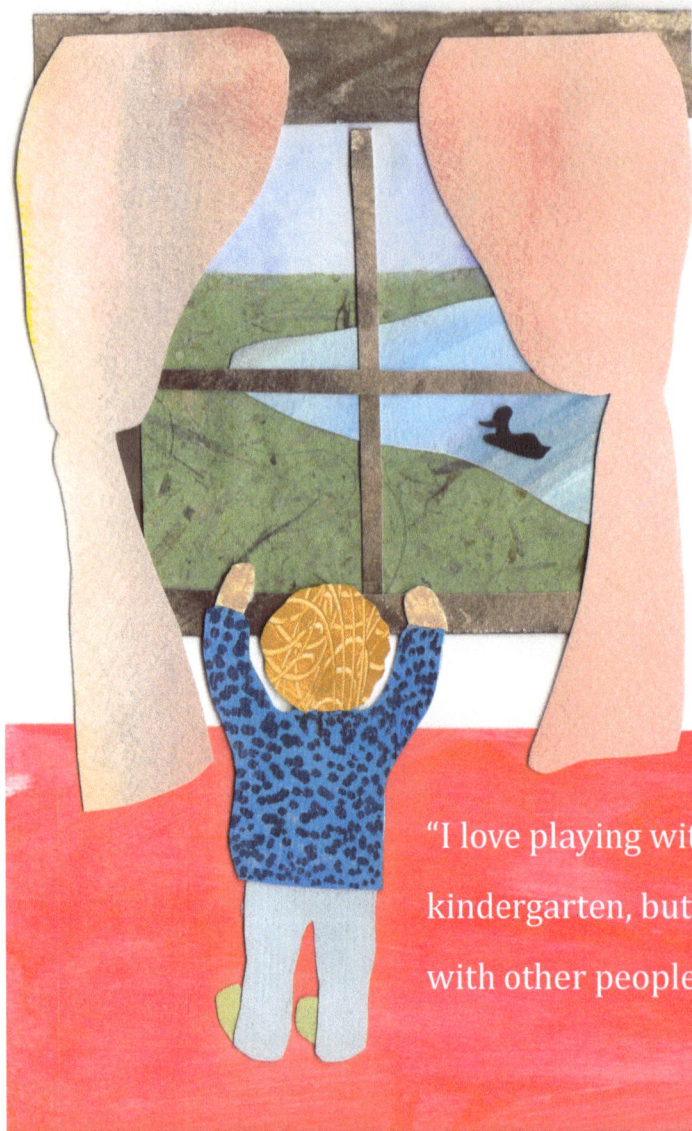

"Sally the OT is here to visit my little brother, Luke," says Leah.

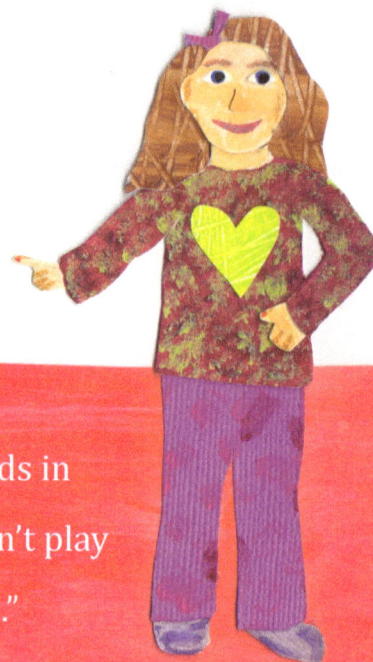

"I love playing with my friends in kindergarten, but Luke doesn't play with other people that much."

Luke and Leah are different,
but they are both happy.
And they both enjoy when
Sally the OT visits.

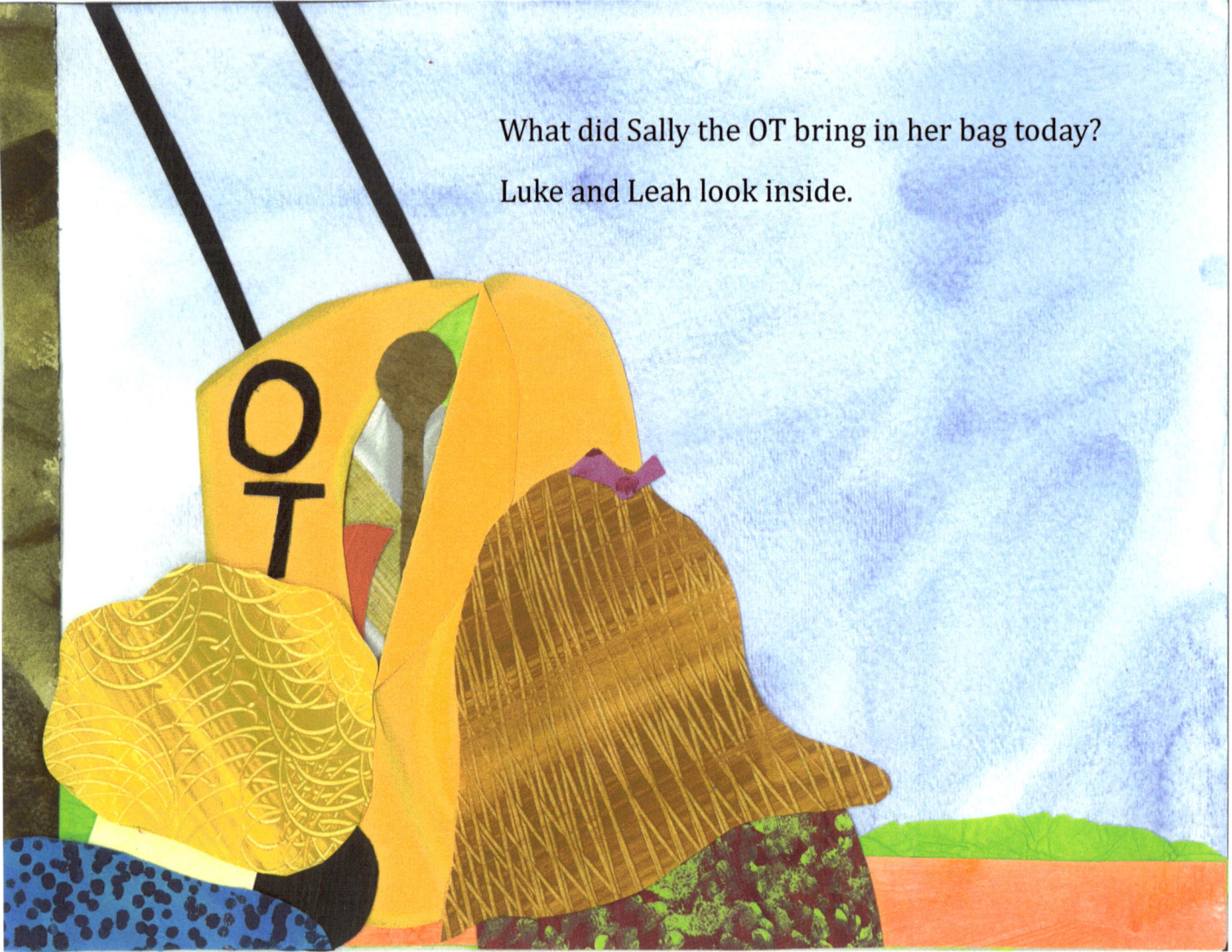

What did Sally the OT bring in her bag today?

Luke and Leah look inside.

They find. . .

A big, red bowl

Three wooden spoons

Measuring cups

Measuring spoons

A rolling pin

And a cookie cutter in the shape of a loon.

Luke reaches for the loon cookie cutter
and holds it in his hand.
Loons are his favorite animal.
Leah likes loons, too.

"Today we are all going to bake cookies together!" Says Sally the OT.

She holds up a picture of the loon-shaped cookies.

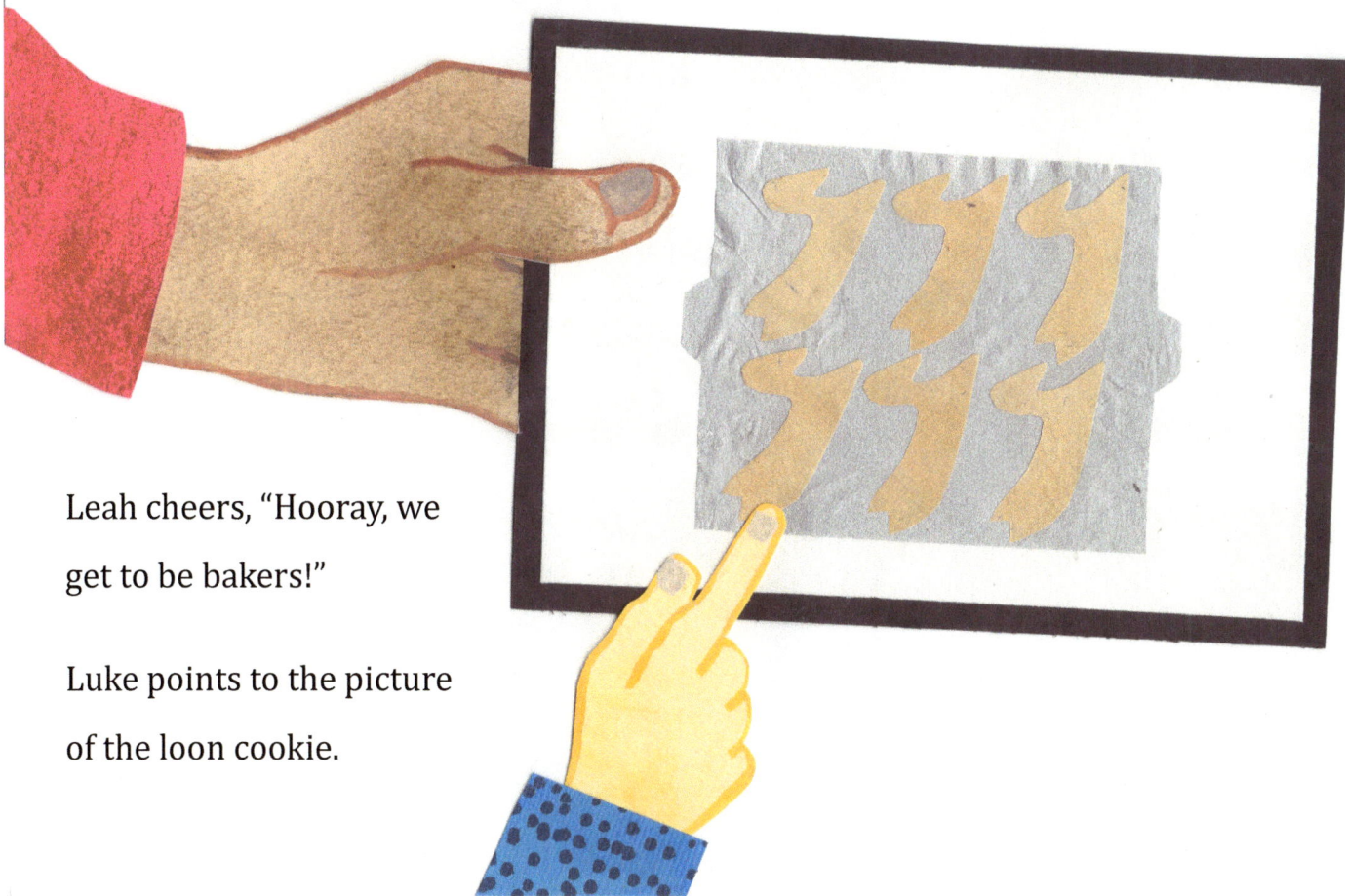

Leah cheers, "Hooray, we get to be bakers!"

Luke points to the picture of the loon cookie.

Time to get started!
The three bakers walk to the
kitchen together.

FLOUR

On a small table in the kitchen, the three bakers find all the ingredients they need.

There is . . .

Sugar

Butter

An Egg

Flour

And Vanilla.

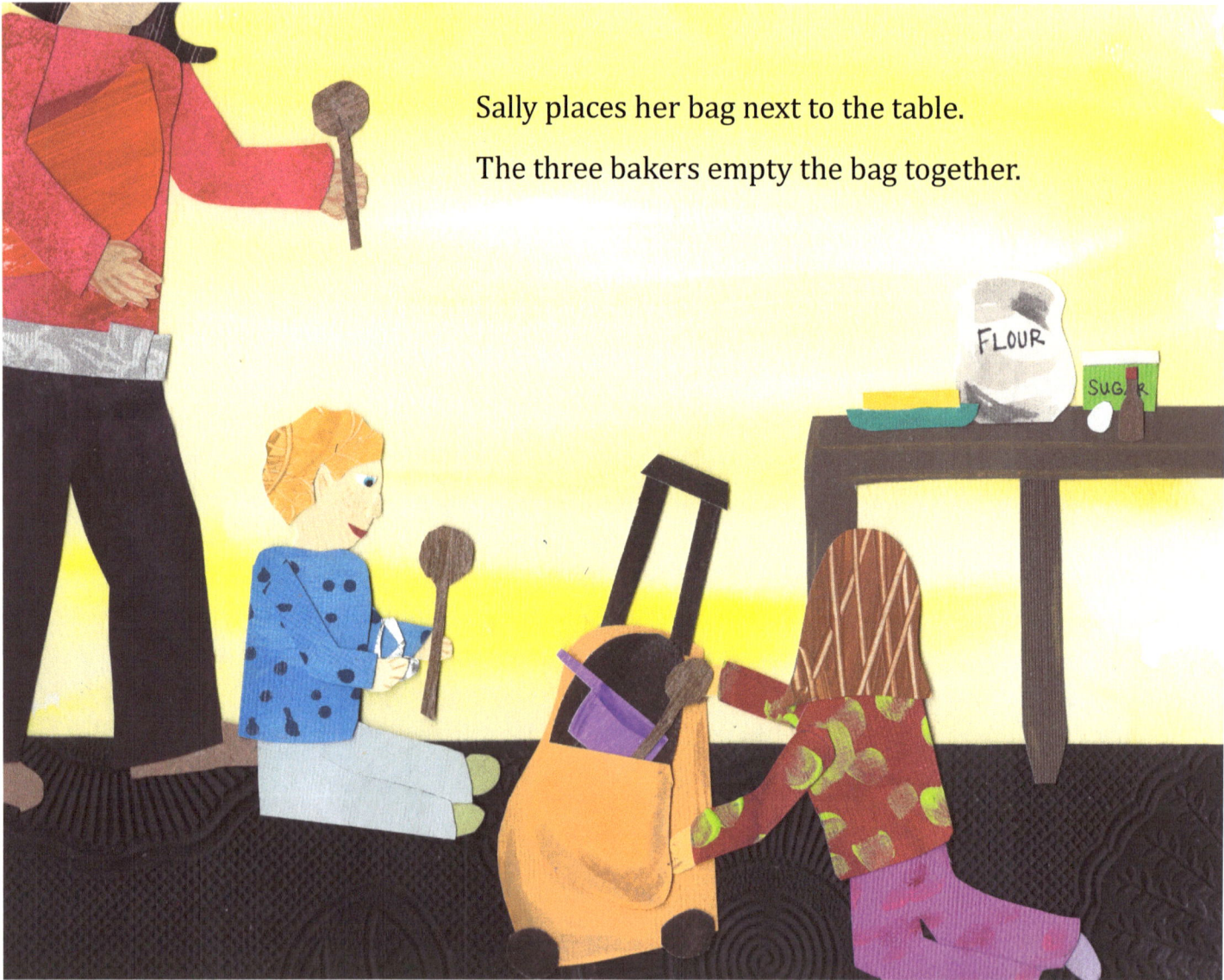

Sally places her bag next to the table.

The three bakers empty the bag together.

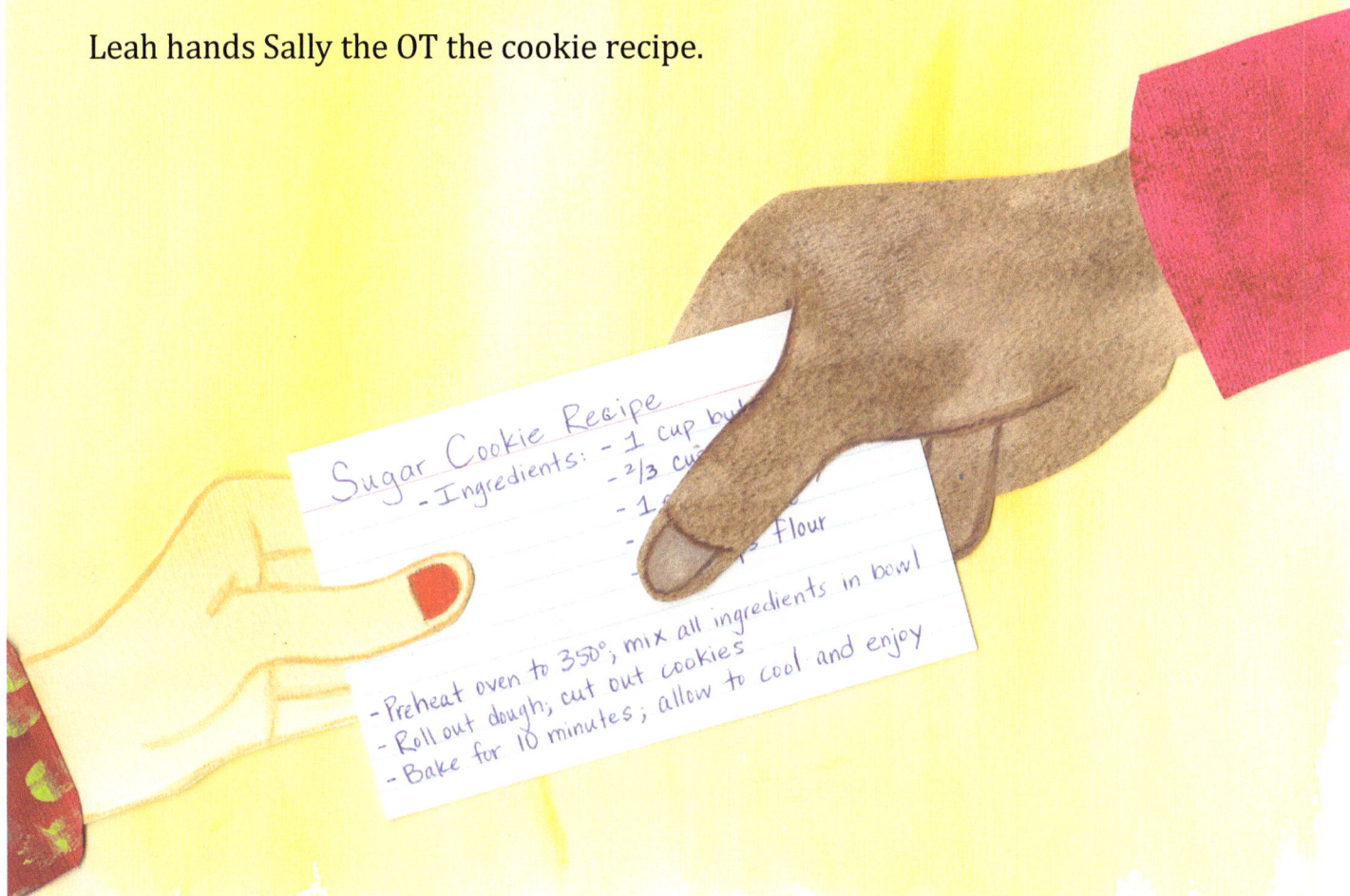

"Mom gave me the cookie recipe! I can read some words, but Luke can't read any. . . He's still learning to talk!" Says Leah.

Leah hands Sally the OT the cookie recipe.

Sugar Cookie Recipe
- Ingredients: - 1 cup bu
- 2/3 cu
- 1
- flour
-
- Preheat oven to 350°; mix all ingredients in bowl
- Roll out dough; cut out cookies
- Bake for 10 minutes; allow to cool and enjoy

Before they start to bake,

The three bakers wash their hands together.

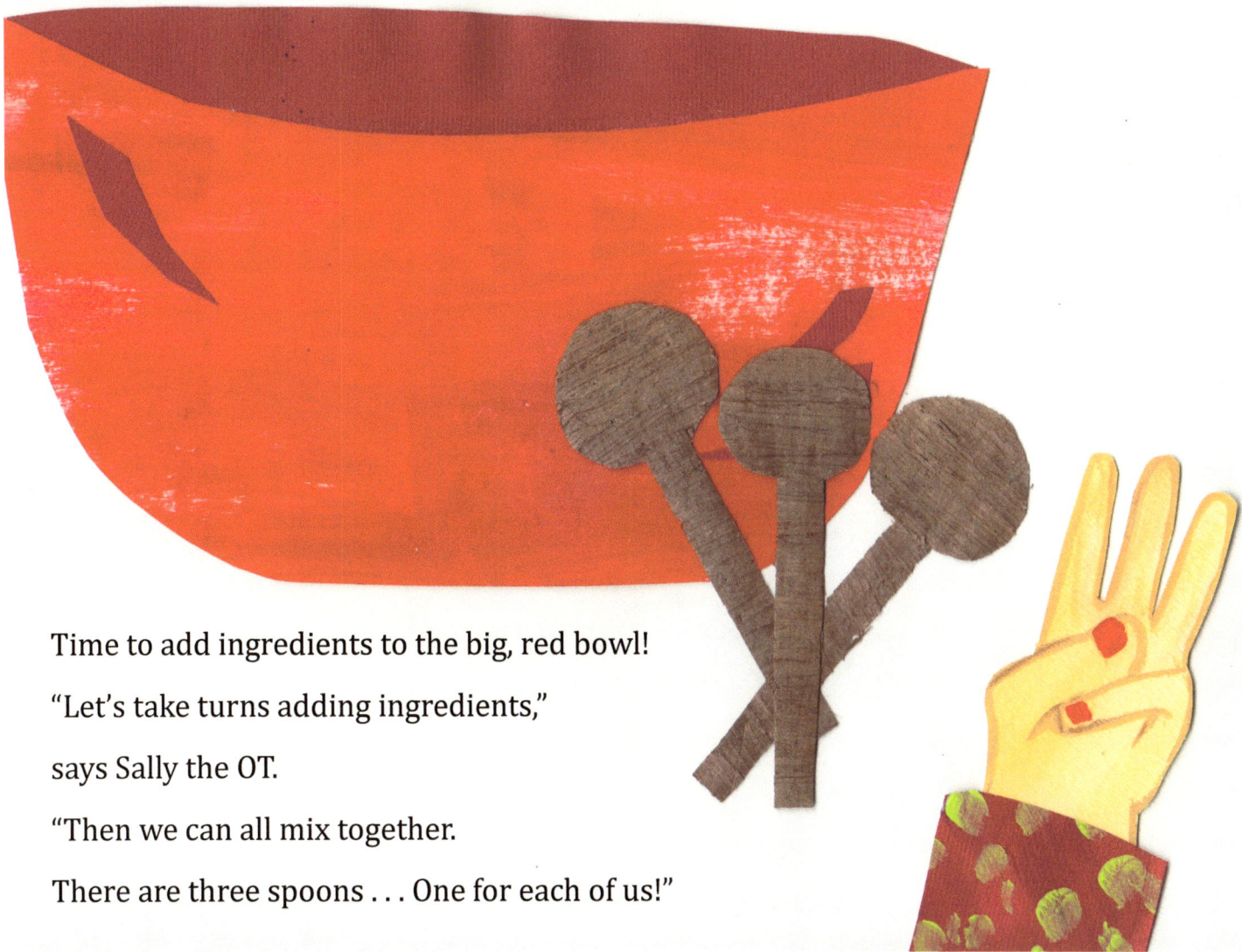

Time to add ingredients to the big, red bowl!

"Let's take turns adding ingredients,"

says Sally the OT.

"Then we can all mix together.

There are three spoons . . . One for each of us!"

First, Luke adds the butter and the sugar . . .

The three bakers mix, mix, and mix together.

Then Sally the OT helps Leah crack
one egg into the bowl . . .
The three bakers mix, mix,
and mix together.

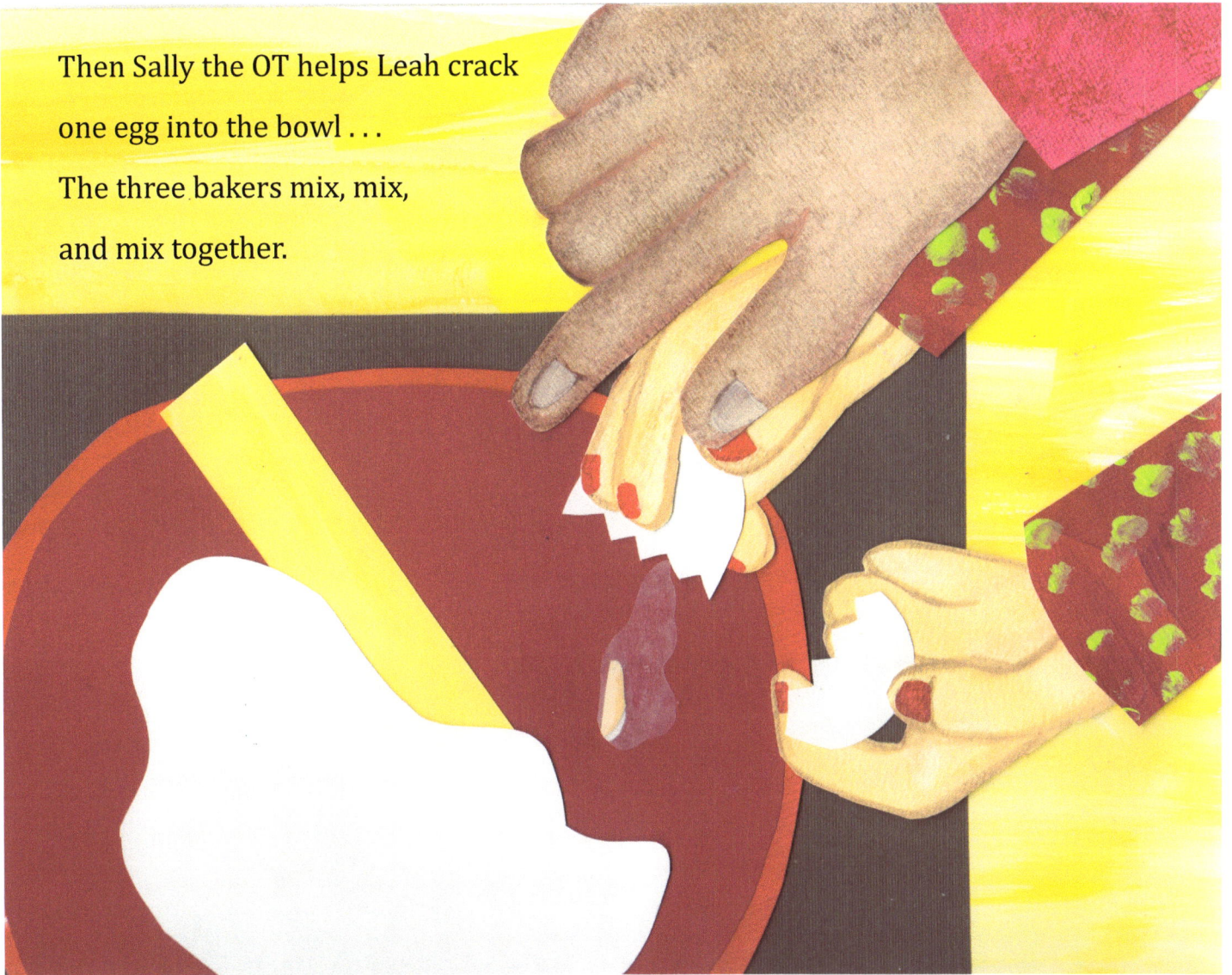

Luke adds the vanilla and Leah adds the flour . . .

The three bakers mix, mix, and mix together.

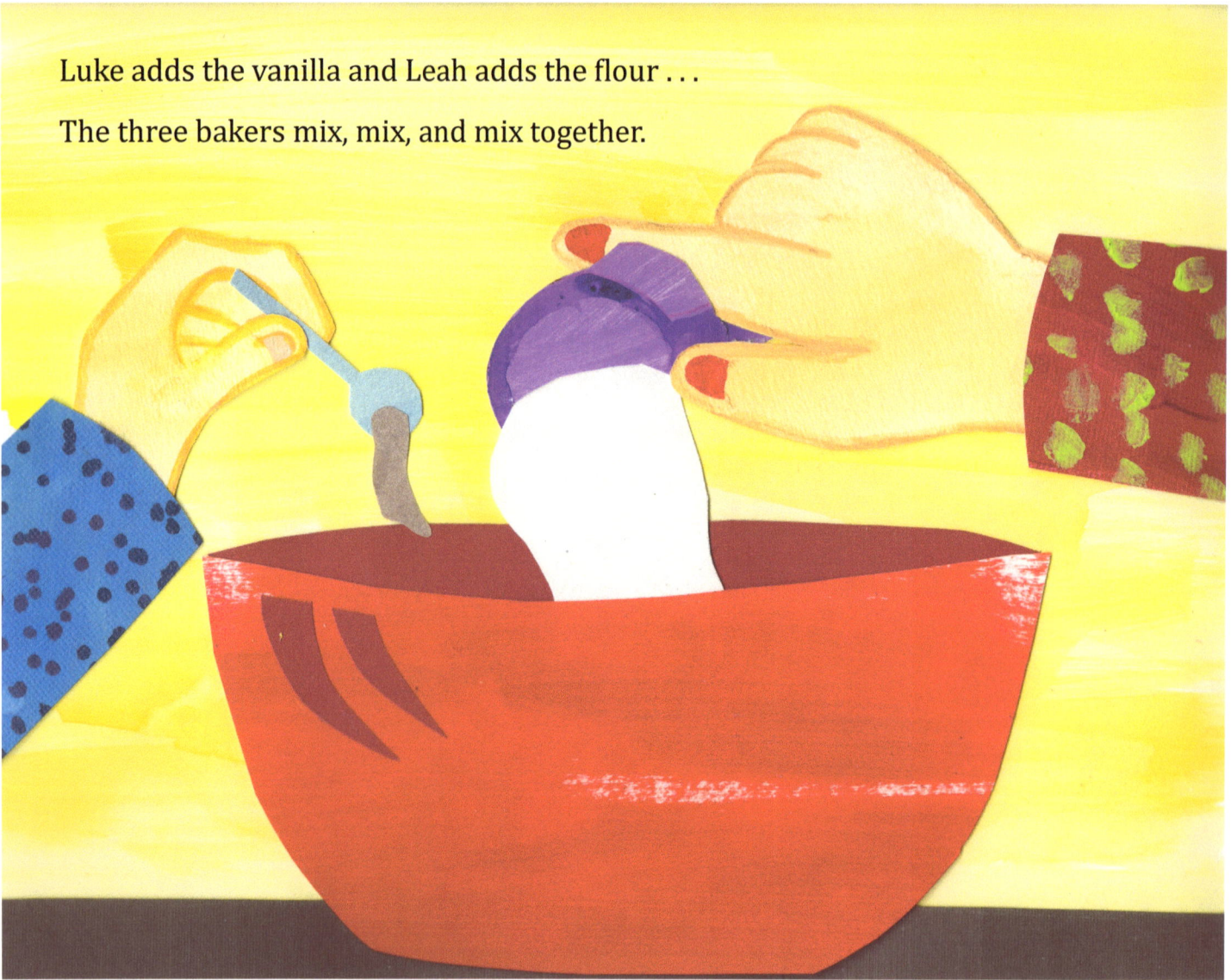

The ingredients mix together to form thick dough.

"We made cookie dough!" Shouts Leah.

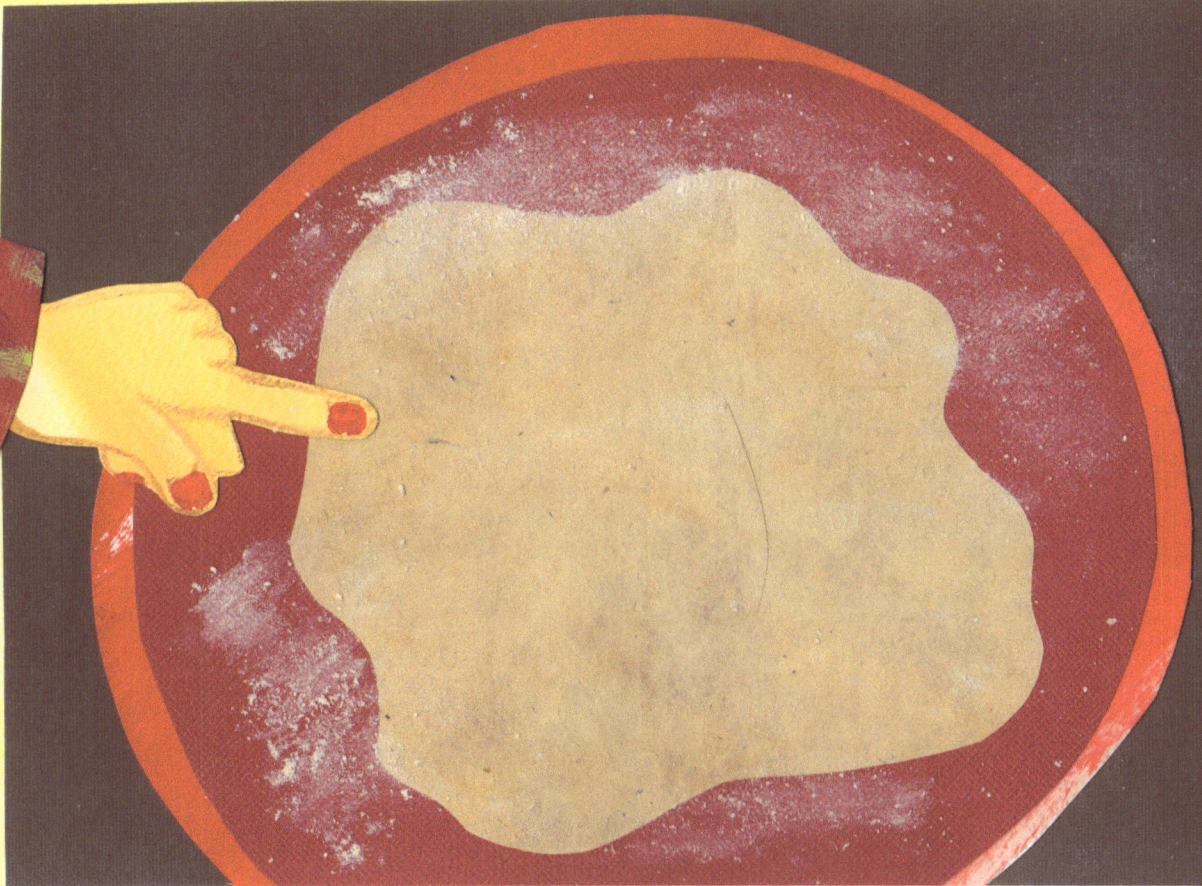

Time to roll the dough nice and flat on the table.

Sally picks up a handful of the dough and places it on the clean tabletop.

"My turn!" Says Leah.

Leah picks up a handful of the dough to add to the pile on the table.

"Luke won't want to touch the dough," explains Leah. "He hates sticky things."

Sally the OT guides Luke's hands toward the sticky dough, and he pulls them away.

"Look, Luke!" Says Sally the OT. She pokes at the dough with her finger.

Poke, poke, poke!

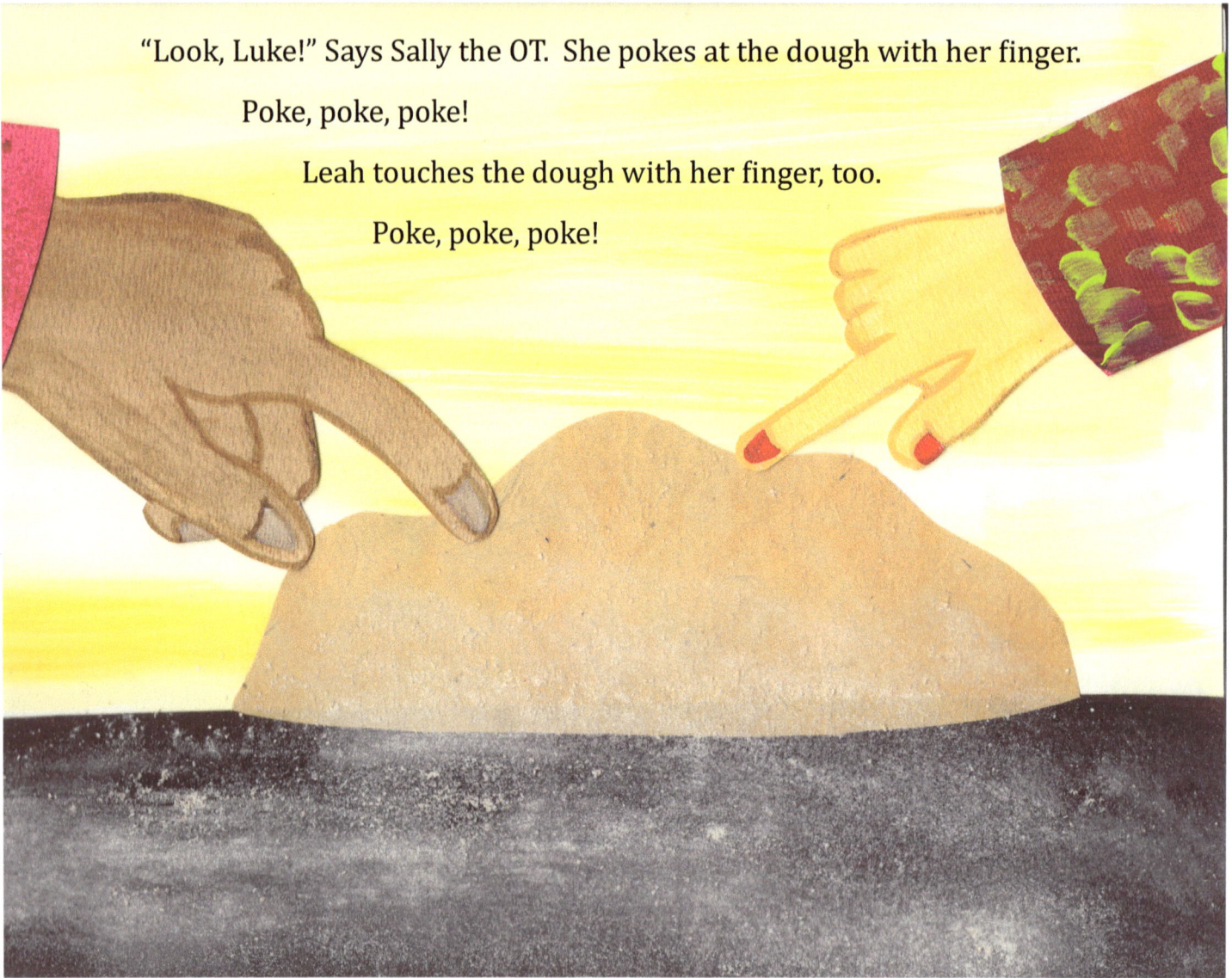

Leah touches the dough with her finger, too.

Poke, poke, poke!

Time for Luke to try.

Luke reaches for the dough and gives it one quick . . . POKE!

"Hooray!" shout Leah and Sally the OT.

Time to use the rolling pin to flatten the dough on the table.

First Sally the OT rolls. Then Leah rolls. Then Luke rolls.

And the three bakers roll together.

"We're ready to cut out our loon shaped cookies," says Sally the OT.

But where did the loon cookie cutter go?

It's not on the table.

It's not in Sally the OT's bag.

Where could it be?

"Looooon, where are you?"
Yells Leah.

Luke points to his pocket.

He slips his hand inside and
pulls out the loon
cookie cutter.

"There it is, you found the
loon!" Exclaims Sally the OT.

The three bakers are ready
to cut out the cookies.

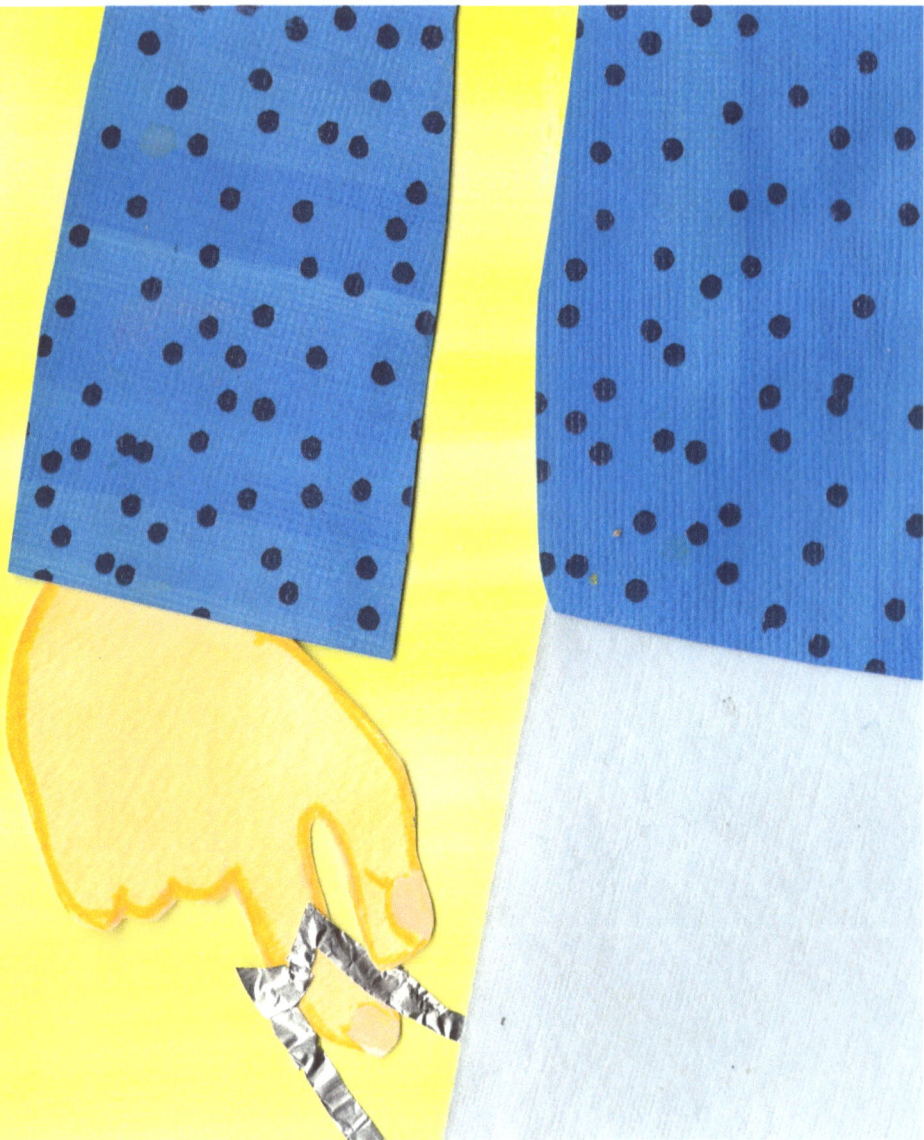

Sally guides Luke's hand to push the loon cookie cutter into the flat cookie dough.

They push, push, and push together.

Then Leah takes a turn with the loon cookie cutter, and so does Sally the OT.

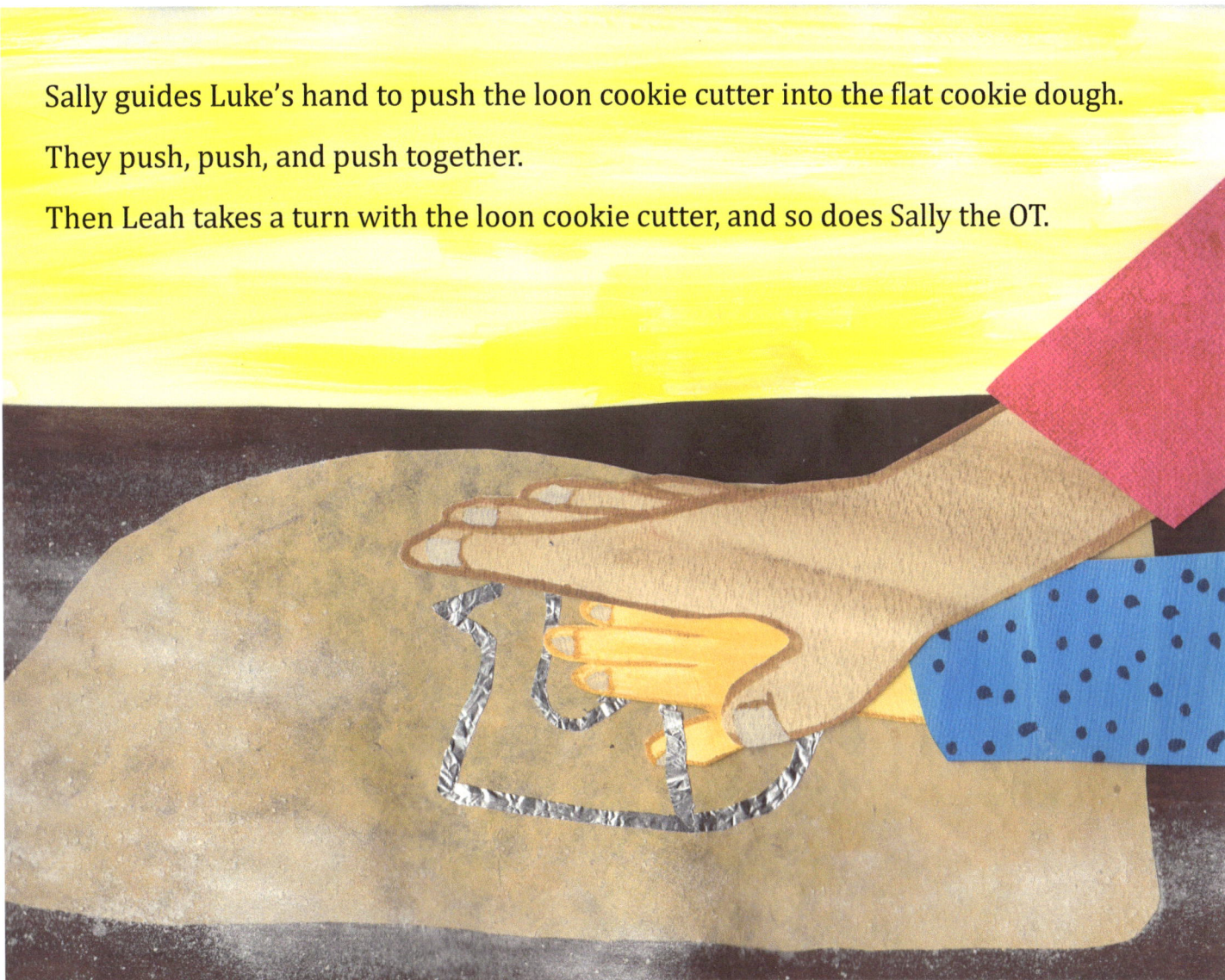

The three bakers help place the cookies
on the baking tray together.

Time to bake the cookies in the oven!

Sally the OT opens the oven door so she can put the tray inside.

Leah sets the timer for 10 minutes.

"Let's clean up while the cookies bake," says Sally.

The three bakers clean up the kitchen together.

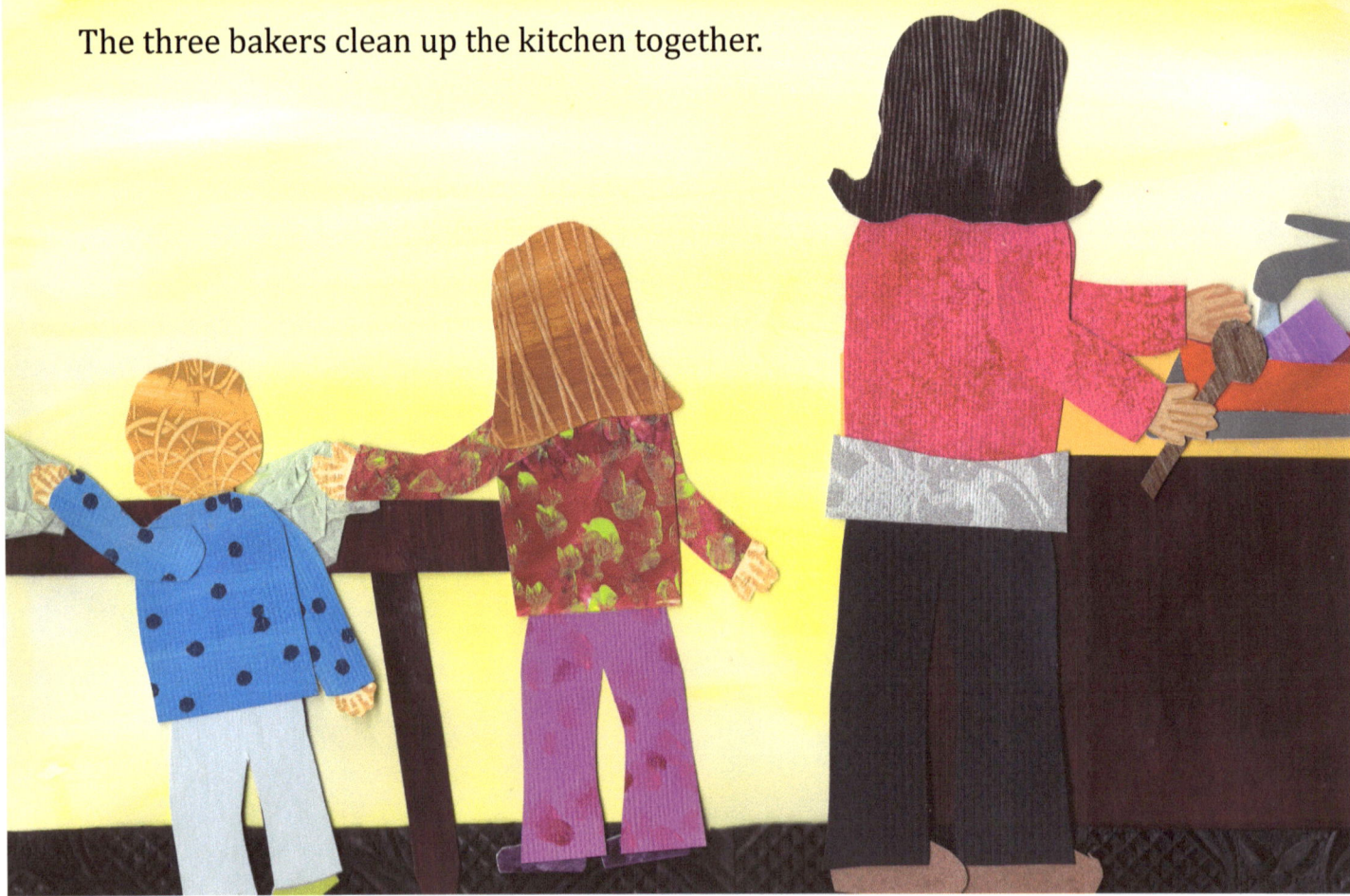

Ding! The timer goes off. The cookies are done!

Sally the OT takes the tray of cookies out of the oven.

She sets the tray on the stovetop to cool.

Once the cookies have cooled, Sally takes three loon cookies from the tray.

She places the cookies on a plate.

Time to eat!

And the three bakers munch, munch, and munch together.

Resources

Definition of Autism: "Autism is a complex developmental disability that typically appears during the first three years of life and affects a person's ability to communicate and interact with others. Autism is defined by a certain set of behaviors and is a "spectrum disorder" that affects individuals differently and to varying degrees. There is no known single cause of autism, but increased awareness and funding can help families today" (http://www.autism-society.org).

Definition of Occupational Therapy (OT): "Occupational therapy is a client-centered health profession concerned with promoting health and well being through occupation. The primary goal of occupational therapy is to enable people to participate successfully in the activities of everyday life" (www.wfot.org).

Definition of Loon: "Loons are migratory birds which breed in forested lakes and large ponds in northern North America and parts of Greenland and Iceland. Their unusual cries, which vary from wails to tremolos to yodels, are distinct to individuals and can be heard at great distances" (http://animals.nationalgeographic.com/animals/birds/common-loon/)

Acknowledgements

I would like to thank my mother for fostering my love of children's books, my Early Intervention co-workers for demonstrating endless compassion, my dedicated graduate school peers for inspiring me with their passion to become therapists, and my professors, specifically Karen, for providing me with endless opportunities to make my dreams become reality. ~AB

Who knew that work could be so much fun? From start to finish, the creation of this book has been a joyful experience working with Allison. I thank my family for always being the wind beneath my wings. ~KJ

The authors extend their thanks to Bob Dugan & Chris Manke for the creation of the e-book version of *Three Bakers & a Loon* which can be found at: http://blogs.bu.edu/kjacobs/

About Us

Allison Boris is a graduate student at Boston University pursuing a master's degree in occupational therapy, and she works in Early Intervention visiting homes of young children with developmental delays and disabilities. She adores children, her family, and living in Boston.

Karen Jacobs is an occupational therapist and ergonomist. She is the proud mother of three children, Laela, Josh & Ariel; and Amma (grandma in Icelandic) to Sophie, Zachary, Liberty & Zane. She loves to spend time with her family at Wakonda Pond in Moultonborough, New Hampshire.

www.ingramcontent.com/pod-product-compliance
Lightning Source LLC
Chambersburg PA
CBHW060853270326
41934CB00002B/119